CRIME SOLVERS

BALLISTICS

by Amy Kortuem

Raintree is an imprint of Capstone Global Library Limited, a company incorporated in England and Wales having its registered office at 264 Banbury Road, Oxford, OX2 7DY – Registered company number: 6695582

www.raintree.co.uk
myorders@raintree.co.uk

Text © Capstone Global Library Limited 2019
The moral rights of the proprietor have been asserted.

Edited by Carrie Braulick Sheely
Designed by Kayla Rossow
Original illustrations © Capstone Global L
Picture research by Svetlana Zhurkin
Production by Kris Wilfahrt
Originated by Capstone Global Library Ltd
Printed and bound in India

ISBN 978 1 4747 7503 8 (hardback)
22 21 20 19 18
10 9 8 7 6 5 4 3 2 1

ISBN 978 1 4747 6334 9 (paperback)
23 22 21 20 19
10 9 8 7 6 5 4 3 2 1

British Library Cataloguing in Publication
A full catalogue record for this book is available from the British Library.

Acknowledgements
We would like to thank the following for permission to reproduce photographs:
Alamy: Pablo Paul, 14; AP Photo: Pool/Post and Courier/Grace Beahm, 29; Dreamstime: Jillvhp, cover; Getty Images: AFP/Tolga Akmen, 18, Corbis/Sandy Huffaker, 19, Los Angeles Times/Rick Loomis, 22–23, The Denver Post/Helen H. Richardson, 13, The Washington Post/Evelyn Hockstein, 9; Newscom: MCT/Gary W. Green, 28, Reuters/Adrees Latif, 5, Zuma Press/Glen Stubbe, 21, Zuma Press/Tampa Bay Times/St. Petersburg Times, 25; Science Source: Louise Murray, 26, Philippe Psaila, 17, Ted Kinsman, 27; Shutterstock: Bjoern Wylezich, 12, Gytis Mikulicius, 15, Hajrudin Hodzic, 7, Microgen, 11, MoiraM, 10. Design Elements by Shutterstock

Every effort has been made to contact copyright holders of material reproduced in this book. Any omissions will be rectified in subsequent printings if notice is given to the publisher.

All the internet addresses (URLs) given in this book were valid at the time of going to press. However, due to the dynamic nature of the internet, some addresses may have changed, or sites may have changed or ceased to exist since publication. While the author and publisher regret any inconvenience this may cause readers, no responsibility for any such changes can be accepted by either the author or the publisher.

CONTENTS

CHAPTER 1

Shots fired!

Workers in a big city hear gunshots. They call the police. A **victim** of a robbery lies injured in the street. The police arrive quickly. They start looking for clues.

FACT

In 2016 criminals used firearms in about 40 per cent of robberies in the United States.

^ Police officers may use torches and other tools to search for clues.

victim person who is hurt, killed or made to suffer

criminal someone who commits a crime

firearm weapon that shoots bullets or other types of ammunition; rifles, handguns and shotguns are firearms

Police officers pick up bullets and **cartridge** cases as **evidence**. Tests show that the bullets came from the gun of a known criminal. **Ballistics** evidence helps to solve another crime.

cartridge container that holds the gunpowder, primer and ammunition for a gun

evidence information, items and facts that help prove something is true or false

ballistics study of firearm evidence in crimes

Cartridge cases left behind can help police to solve crimes involving firearms.

CHAPTER 2

Gathering evidence

Ballistics includes the study of guns, bullets and the paths that bullets take. Ballistics information helps police to find out how shootings happened. Crime **scene** investigators (**CSI**s) gather ballistics evidence.

scene place of an event or action

CSI police officer who finds evidence at crime scenes; in the UK these officers are called Scene of Crime Officers (SOCOs)

⌄ A CSI holds a cartridge case found at a crime scene.

⌄ A CSI studies a gun found at a crime scene.

CSIs look for guns left behind at the scene of a crime. Sometimes they can find out who owns a gun. They may find **fingerprints** and other evidence on guns.

A lab worker brushes metal powder on a gun to check for fingerprints. The powder sticks to fingerprints to make them appear.

fingerprint pattern made by the curved ridges on the tips of your fingers

CSIs also look for bullets and
cartridge cases at crime scenes.
They mark where everything was found.
CSIs take photos of what they find.

FACT Even small pieces of bullets can tell police about the gun used in a crime.

CSIs look for cartridge cases and other evidence at a crime scene in Colorado, USA.

CSIs gather the guns, bullets and other evidence. They carefully place items in paper or cardboard containers. They pack bullets and guns separately. They take the items to a crime lab.

Sometimes bullets get stuck in surfaces. CSIs may cut out pieces of walls or floors that have bullets in them. They then take the pieces to the lab.

CHAPTER 3

Comparing bullets and cartridge cases

When fired, a gun makes marks on bullets and cartridge cases. Police can use the marks to match guns with bullets and cases from crime scenes. To find a match, firearms examiners load a gun and fire it.

➤ A firearms examiner gets ready to fire a gun in a lab.
The metal container holds a material that will stop the bullet.

FACT

Bullet markings are called striations.

Examiners then look at
the marks on the test bullet or
cartridge case. They compare them
with the ones on the bullet or case
from the crime scene. They see if
the marks match.

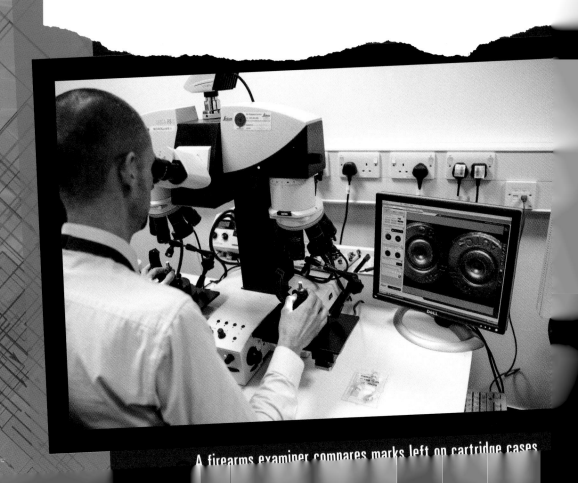

A firearms examiner compares marks left on cartridge cases.

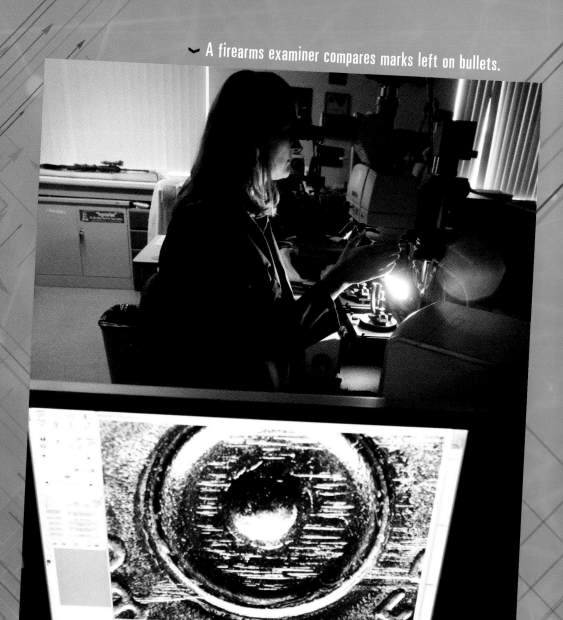

➤ A firearms examiner compares marks left on bullets.

FACT Henry Goddard, a British police officer in the 1800s, was the first to trace a bullet back to the gun that fired it.

19

Some labs have a ballistics **database**. Staff at the lab enter a bullet or cartridge case image into the database. The computer then searches for matches from past crime scenes.

database collection of organized information on a computer

A firearms expert in the United States uses a national ballistics database. He places two images side by side to help compare them.

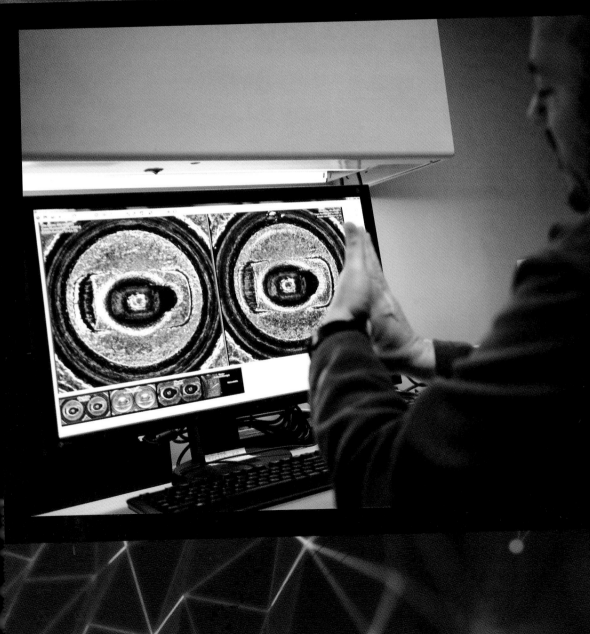

CHAPTER 4

Other firearm evidence

When a gun is fired, the burning gunpowder creates gunshot residue (GSR). GSR can spray several metres. CSIs look for GSR. It can tell them where people were during a crime.

A police officer (left) checks a person's hands for GSR at a crime scene.

CSIs study the paths of bullets to learn how a shooting happened. CSIs search crime scenes for bullet entrance and exit holes. They sometimes put rods through the holes to find a bullet's path.

FACT

When a gun fires, it can suck in tiny bits of hair, blood or fabric. This material is called backspatter. Police can use it as evidence.

A police expert studies metal rods placed in a car to find the paths of bullets.

A line shows the bullet's path on this crime scene map.

Firearms examiners sometimes map crime scenes using computers. The maps can show bullet paths. They can also show victim or shooter locations.

On average, bullets travel at a speed of
762 metres (2,500 feet) per second.

Firearms examiners may talk about their findings in court. They explain the evidence. Ballistics is an important crime-solving tool.

A CSI shows a gun in court that was collected as evidence.

∧ A ballistics expert (right) explains
gun-related evidence in court.

GLOSSARY

ballistics study of firearm evidence in crimes

cartridge container that holds the gunpowder, primer and ammunition for a gun

criminal someone who commits a crime

CSI police officer who finds evidence at crime scenes; in the UK these officers are called Scene of Crime Officers (SOCOs)

database collection of organized information on a computer

evidence information, items and facts that help prove something is true or false; criminal evidence can be used in court cases

fingerprint pattern made by the curved ridges on the tips of your fingers

firearm weapon that shoots bullets or other types of ammunition

scene place of an event or action

striation streak on a bullet; each gun leaves a different striation mark on a bullet

victim person who is hurt, killed or made to suffer

FIND OUT MORE

BOOKS

Crime-Fighting Devices (Science and Technology), Robert Snedden (Raintree, 2012)

Crime Scene Detective, Carey Scott (Dorling Kindersley, 2007)

Fighting Crime (Heroic Jobs), Ellen Labrecque (Raintree, 2013)

Forensic Science (DK Eyewitness Books), DK (Dorling Kindersley, 2008)

WEBSITE

www.connectionsacademy.com/resources/ instructographics/fingerprinting

Try this fingerprinting activity in your own home!

COMPREHENSION QUESTIONS

1. Sometimes CSIs can't find guns, bullets or cartridge cases at a crime scene. What other evidence can they look for to solve crimes?

2. What does gunshot residue at a crime scene tell police?

3. How do ballistics databases help firearms examiners?

INDEX